My Name is Kym

KYMBERLY TWYMAN MCENHEIMER
JUANITA TWYMAN, EDITOR

urbanpress

My Name is Kym
by Kymberly Twyman McEnheimer
Copyright ©2021 Juanita Twyman

ISBN 978-1-63360-163-5

For Worldwide Distribution
Printed in the U.S.A.

Urban Press
P.O. Box 8881
Pittsburgh, PA 15221-0881
412.646.2780
www.urbanpress.us

Table of Contents

Preface

"I created you in my own image
with My special blessing"
(Genesis 1:27-28).

Hello, my name is Juanita Twyman, mother of Kymberly Shawn Twyman McEnheimer and I would like to share a little about my daughter before you read her essays and poems in the pages that follow.

Who is Kymberly (Kym) Twyman McEnheimer?

Kym was a nice, kind, sweet, quiet, girl. As an only child, she was very special to my husband, Gerry, and me. She was shy but could speak her mind eloquently on paper. Kym loved reading and many times got lost in her writing. As a child, she was fascinated with bedtime stories. We enrolled her in a book club which helped to feed her gift for writing. In college, she majored in English. This catapulted her writing talents to another level as she expressed her gift to develop imagery in her writing as she crafted a person, place, or thing—to enthrall her readers through her stories. It was without a doubt a special blessing given to her.

Kym always knew what she wanted to do. She did not like being an only child but loved her parents and her family. Others often thought she was soft and she was. However, as her parents, we knew that this softness was exactly what also made her very strong. She experienced much happiness and openly loved others. No greater love was given to her than the gift of her two sons, Shaine and Kyle.

Kym's Achievements

Kym won awards and was recognized for her writing throughout her school years.

1. National Library of Poetry (Editors Choice Award 1997) ("A Lasting Mirage")
2. National Poetry Press ("Young American Sings")

3. Peabody High School Seniors Essay Contest — First and second place in an area-wide essay of Westminster College and the Black Student Union in observance Dr. Martin Luther King Jr.'s accomplishments ("Is There Freedom?")

4. Member of Carnegie Library Poetry Forum Outstanding Achievement at Peabody High School ("The Halls Are Alive with the Sounds of Music")

5. Member of the Alpha Kappa Alpha Sorority, Inc.

6. Active member of St. James AME Church where she participated in: Young People Department (YPD), Young People Adult Choir, and an active member of Sister to Sister Church School.

After graduating from Peabody High School in east Pittsburgh, Kym was accepted to Duquesne University in 1977 where she earned Dean's List honors and graduated in 1981 with a degree in English and a minor in psychology and communications. Kym's writing experiences included recognition in The Duquesne University Magazine, The Eye (a quarterly publication sponsored by Inner-City Services of Carnegie Library), and Young America Sings, an annual anthology of poems by high school students sponsored by The National Poetry Press. She was also a master of arts candidate in the graduate communications program. Kym was employed by Zurich Insurance Company of Pittsburgh as a worker's compensation claims specialist.

Education was important to Kym and our family and we are please that both Kym's sons have graduated from college. Shaine graduated from California University of Pa in 2010, with a Bachelor of Science in Business Administration. Her youngest son Kyle graduated from Alabama State University of Montgomery Alabama in 2013 with a Bachelor of Science Degree in Criminal Justice. I know Kym would be proud of their accomplishments.

Why Is the Timing Right for This Book?

"But do not forget this one thing, dear friends:
With the Lord a day is like a thousand years,
and a thousand years are like one day" (2 Peter 3:8).

I look up and it has been twenty years since Kym left us to be with the Lord on June 13, 2001. It is still unbelievable, but I know its true. From a small child, I knew she was a writer. I also knew as an adult woman, Kym continued to pour her soul into her writings and left many journals as evidence. I could not bring myself to pick them up to read. It hurt just to see her handwriting—until now.

Nothing can ever replace my daughter and no words can express my thoughts or the depth of my love for her. However, she lives on with me through her sons. As they have matured, I know she would be proud of the men they have become as I am. As the healing began, I wanted them to know more of what I knew about Kym as her mother who had witnessed her love for words, I wanted them to know more about her through her writings. At one point several years ago, I picked them up but could not go through with this project Then one day I found that I could. Her literary work and world then began to unfold to me in ways I could not have imagined.

When is the right time to create a compilation of her writings? Bad time? Good time? Then I thought, "Why not? Why not let the rest of our family, friends, and those we don't know be blessed through her writings? Who knows? Kym's reflections on real-life issues may help someone else. One just never knows. Such a gift is meant to be shared, not hidden away. "

You might think it seems strange that after 20 years, I choose to reveal the strength and character of my daughter. Truth be told, I didn't plan this as an anniversary release. It is 2021 as I write and it just happened that way. After reading the memories she left behind in her poems and short stories, I learned so much from her and about her. Upon the release of this book, family members who recall Kym's shyness will be surprised at the depth of this remarkable young woman who left us at the all-too-young age of 42.

She had the uncanny ability to vividly paint a picture from multiple vantage points and experiences that contributed to what she unfolds for you, her audience. As I went through her material, I was drawn to read on and it became a need for me to release portions of this, her legacy. I felt others should also learn more about what was on her mind. These writings are part of her life, a short life well-lived—a life that I have chosen to celebrate. An ambitious, smart young woman, I was surprised by her words of wisdom. Through her own words, Kym's soul will be revealed to you in these pages, strongly crafted and powerful. She imparts to us a vision bigger than her own life.

I want to believe she left this for us to read. Often Kym said she wanted to be a writer and would have been qualified to do so. Only children have time to reflect and think. In addition to her love of school, Kym was interested in the arts, to include lessons in violin, piano, and ballet, all experiences expressed through her writings.

Simply put, this is a book about my daughter who had joys, heartaches, and disappointments like any young beautiful black girl who was living and navigating life. She was loved and early in life had anything a poor black girl could have. Kym married in 1984 and had two sons—Shaine and Kyle—who you will hear from at the end of this book.

Why not remember your loved ones especially the one you birthed? Whether one year or twenty years, there is no difference in the love I have for her. I never want to remember her with the typical fanfare that people display, like memorial flowers on an altar on special occasions. I respect those who choose to do that. As for me, I choose to remember Kym through the gift of her own words, a gift that will continue to live on. Be touched. Be blessed. See yourself in her writings. Hear your life experiences echoing through her words. Know that you are not alone as you go through the ups and downs on this journey called life.

We hope you will enjoy reading this book, a mother's tribute to her daughter as I compiled what she left undone. Kym chose me to gather a collection of her writings to share with others. Who else could she entrust to do so? Our love remains forever unbreakable. I will enjoy her published contribution to the world along with my grandsons for years to come. And now I invite you to enjoy *My Name Is Kym.*

Juanita Twyman
Kym's Mother
Pittsburgh, PA
May 2021

My Name is Kym

This book is dedicated to Kym's sons—
Shaine C. McEnheimer
and
Kyle E. McEnheimer

Kym celebrating her mom's 62nd birthday

Kym's Introduction

Hi! My name is Kim Twyman. There are so many things to tell you about myself that I don't know where to begin. Well, first of all, I make friends with almost anyone—animals included. I have a strong interest in domestic animals. Perhaps one day I may like wild bears and lions but for right now, my main concern is gentle animals. Baby animals appeal to me the most for I am very sympathetic and will gladly take a stray kitten or puppy home even if my mother doesn't care for them as much.

In my spare time at home, I find thousands of things to do in an hour. I am a true Gemini and cannot stay busy with one thing over a long period of time. Sometimes I'll watch TV for a few hours until I get bored, which on some days is sooner than others. I like to play records. Lately I've been in the mood for soft, slow music, but at least twice a week I'll be playing all fast music and acting as wild as ever. Something that I have been doing a lot this week is drawing. I have always had an interest in art since about first grade. Mostly I draw little people in everyday life. Sometimes I write a few words about them like an illustrated story. Other times I believe I'd like to be a fashion designer and, taking today's styles, draw them on model people. Sometimes I even color them in and put estimated price tags on the garments.

One of my strongest interests, even more so than art, is writing. As far back as I can remember I have been writing long and short stories. Along with my newer ones, I have stories at home that I have written in first or second grade on up. Of course, the old ones are not as good and complicated as my newer ones, but I still take them out on rainy days to read and enjoy the simple way they are put together. I had thought about correcting them, adding things, and changing them, but I decided to leave them as they are so when I am much older, I can look back on them and compare how I wrote each year. I have a folder full of my recent stories which I take out often to make changes. Sometime soon I hope to send them to a publisher for evaluation.

Of course, I can go on and on with all of my interests, but you may have found me boring already. I never like to tell anyone everything about me for when they talk to me there won't be anything that they don't know, and I'm the kind of person who likes to surprise people with something new. I like to change, so that there will always be something that I didn't know and the fun of it is to discover it. Of course, I don't like to change too quickly. There are always little things that I would like to stay just as it was.

Kym Twyman

Kym's
Reflections

Life Is a Trip . . .

Life is a trip . . .
   A dizzy merry-go-round revolving in polluted air.
Disjointed cycles that repeat themselves
   at unexpected times.
No one desires to get off;
   they must be afraid, or so I think.
The crumbled ground below
   is a step that too few take.
The monotonous game,
   lacking a winner,
     overcrowded with losers.
A mind disease,
      a ride to nowhere.
  a spinning journey of wasted dreams
without a beginning
      and incapable
  of ever developing
     a sensible ending.

Pain expressed in a thousand words,
  A vibrating sensation teetering
     on the brink of instability.
A feeling, incapable of expression
     for it refuses understanding
  and relishes confusion.
The delights of perplexity—
  a mind in chaos,
yet this legitimate pain—
     is graceless and sincere.

Experience the beauty of man's
    captivating love.
  Swim in the passionate waters
    of sensuality.
    Bittersweet lust, hard-core desire;
      desperately clinging to the
moist, body heat, filled with the
  burning intensity of nature's
  whirlpool.

I no longer know what I write.
 I am not the striving poet of tomorrow,
  but the dark shadow who hides
   in the corner of yesterday.
What I shall become has been my quest,
 yet the answers do not seek
   my company.
            I can hear the laughter,
      Visualize the scorn.
   Tears flow with ease,
     Shoulders droop in failure
       But . . . I shall trudge on
Life's hardships,
      a writer's dilemma
must be temporary.
  I must maintain my dream
       I must

          overpower
          and

                  conquer.
The awaited day is becoming a reality.
The appointed time is no longer a faded dream
The special hour,
The enchanted second,
   the realization that I shall no longer
   walk through the ageless halls,
   study within the smoke-filled room
     amid the hub-bub of intoxicated laughter,
     and the naked sensuality
        of lustful music.
I shall no longer encounter the
   meaningless love-affairs
  that intwine the passionate body
   in a web that has no true feelings,
     only momentous desires
       flung out and never to invade again.
             Never to return to
       what was never real.
        I'm finally awakening from the ill-conceived nightmare,
Refreshed, reconciled
       and purge . . . cleansed
  in the cool waters
     of life's ecstasy.

Kymberly Twyman McEnheimer

My Lifetime Goal

My lifetime goal is to make people happy.
I can feel the warm radiance of their smiles in my endless dark world.
I can feel the deep vibrations as they rock to the beat and sing along
with me.
I can only offer the simple gift of music to the land of my people.
I have built the foundation; take it to the unlimited heights of your
minds.

My messages are clear as I spend a little time and share a little love
with those who need to feel the spirit within them.
I have the power to move you—if you 're willing.
Music is my language, it's a universal sound that all who hear can
understand.
Through my music I can gather all of the beautiful people of this
world.
Let us join hands and feel that spirit around the globe.
Together we can sing the songs in the Key of Life.

My Name is Kym

The Camp Fire Experience

When I recall my days in the Camp Fire organization, a lot of things come to my mind—the camps, the trips, the friendships, and the overall experiences that I truly believe have helped shape me into the woman I am today.

I started out in the organization in grade school. There was a big focus on the history of Camp Fire, earning beads, doing good deeds such as singing in nursing homes, and volunteering our services to the community.

In later years, we experienced the residential camps. These were not as fun, but the memories are there of hiking, boating, nature walks, and sleeping in tents. I was also involved in the day camps which were also activity-filled, and during my teen years, we were able to help out as assistant leaders.

I think my most treasured memories of Camp Fire were the trips to Washington, D.C., twice to New York to see Broadway plays, and even to Toronto, Canada. The highlight of our trips was the one to the island of Eleuthera in the Bahamas on a cultural exchange program for two weeks in the summer of 1977. This was an unforgettable experience in which we lived on the island and experienced every aspect of the culture.

When I was in college, I became a leader of Blue Birds, the six-year-olds, for about two years. This was a lot of fun because I was able to "give back" what I knew and learned from my days as a young Camp Fire girl.

Today, I am the mother of two boys, so there will be no future Blue Birds or Camp Fire girls. But I do feel that growing up in the Camp Fire organization, forming lifetime friendships, learning to respect others, and to carry myself with respect and dignity have indeed made me a more secure person. I find that many of the decisions that I have made in my life have been influenced by the things I was taught by my leaders. It will always remain an unforgettable experience, and I truly believe that Camp Fire girls never fade. They may grow older, they may have their ups and downs, but like me, they still remember with a smile those wonderful days, and know if they had to do it all again, they would.

Kym (top left) as a Camp Fire Girl

Island of Eleuthera
Bahamas 1977

Eleuthera can never be home
can never be a place for familiar eyes, and yet I wanted it to be—
at least for a little while,
at least for a day, a week.
I loved its beaches of crystal pink sand.
I loved its irregularly shaped seashells
and aquamarine waters
can never be home.
I loved its warm, loving people that
shared a dream—I never knew.
That felt a deep pride I never experienced
that held a feeling I never understood—
can never be home.
Yet I wished it could be
for a little while,
for eternity is not that long.

Young Kym's Short Essays

A Fish Out of Water

One afternoon, I decided to change my fishbowl. I had two guppies at that time. One was a girl and the other was a boy. His tail was blue, orange, green, and yellow. I liked him ever so much. So that day, I decided to change their water.

I called my kitten, Babydoll, and together we went down in our basement. I carried the bowl downstairs. She and I hunted for something to put them in while I washed the bowl. All I could find was a little plastic container. The sides were low, but it would do. I put both fish in it with some water. All went well, at least I thought it did.

I washed the bowl. Then I looked in the container. And there was only one fish in the container. I looked around. On the floor was the boy fish, my favorite one! I started to scream and ran skipping steps upstairs. I told my mother. We rushed down and mother scooped the fish in the water. "Boy," I sighed, "that was close."

Changing Fish

1. Decide upon
2. Change the fish
3. Find fish is gone
4. Go get mother
5. Fish is saved

Kym with Donna, her lifelong friend

A Short Story About the Fairy

English 2
September 25, 1974
(15 years old)

My crystal moment is something that keeps me in awe and mystery even today. When I tell my story, most people don't believe me and say that I am only imagining it. I don't like to think of it as that, though what they say sounds quite logical. If so, then why do I repeatedly wonder about it? Well, let me go on and tell you about it, for I've kept you in suspense long enough.

I'm not too sure if this is a crystal moment, but it happened at a time when I was about seven or eight. I lost a tooth and as my parents had always taught me, I put it under my pillow for the tooth fairy. Usually, I expected a quarter or two per tooth which pleased me very much. When I awoke the next morning, my tooth was still there. I was much surprised and quite upset about the matter for I had expected money. I got out of bed (the tooth was still under my pillow) and went out into the hall for about two minutes to be exact. No one entered my room, I am very sure of that, but when I returned and removed my pillow, there was a new shiny quarter and the tooth was gone! The quarter was still warm as If someone had just finished holding it. I stood there absolutely aghast not knowing what to make of this miracle, as I like to call it.

Many people ask me over and over again if I am sure no one entered my room. Yes, I am sure, for I stood in the hall right outside. This is something I never have been able to explain for as I grew older, I learned that it is usually the mother or father who takes the tooth and replaces it with money.

Who, how, and why, I cannot explain to this very day and I imagine for the rest of my life, I shall wonder if there really is a tooth fairy?

Bill's Window Mistake

May 20, 1969
(9 years old)

Early one morning when the sun was not quite high in the sky, Michael Suden went visiting. He was in the mood to play ball. He went to four houses. By then he had a lot of boys.

"What shall we play?" asked a boy named Sam. "Let's play baseball," suggested Fattie. The others agreed. There were seven boys, but seven was not an even number. Someone would not have to play. They all decided Fattie should be the one. Fattie cried as he left. Now the teams were even.

Michael and Bill were team captains. Bill was at bat. He hit a high fly ball. The ball was headed for the window. It broke the window. Mr. Snow came out ever so angry. Bill apologized and Mr. Snow could not help laughing. "It's alright," he said. Bill was so relieved!

Catching Worms

One July day, my neighbor and I were playing. His name was Carlton. We each had a jar. I ran to get a shovel. I came back with nothing. "I couldn't find one, Carlton," I said. "Well, never mind. We can use sticks," Carlton replied. So I sat down beside him. He gave me a stick and we began to dig. After awhile, I gave a shout, "I got one!" Carlton ran to see. It was a baby worm no bigger than your baby finger. I held it in my hands. "What shall I name it, Carlton?" Carlton stood still while trying to think. Finally, he said, "I think his name should be Percy." I agreed and put him in a jar.

Carlton sat down to dig while I fed the worm turtle food. The stick broke so Carlton got another. Then I heard a voice say, "Carlton, it's time to go." Carlton looked up. He handed me a red worm. "Goodbye. I can't keep worms anyway. Mother's afraid of them!"

Nine-year-old Kym on Easter Sunday

Fun in the Summertime

Hurrah! Summer has arrived. Let's play a game. Okay, Let's play tennis! Here, take a racket. Let's begin. Back and forth goes the ball. What fun! We could play forever!

Let's go on a picnic. I will pack hotdogs and ham sandwiches and cookies. Let's go out in the country! We'll find a nice spot and sit down. Have a sandwich. Picnics are fun. We must go but we had a nice time.

Now we are at a beach. Ah! Sit down, sit down in the sand. Let's make a castle. Look at the waves. What fun it is out here. We gather seashells. I found a nice one. It is red, blue, white and green. Look, a sea crab! We have such a nice time.

Now we are home. Just relax. I will get a blanket. Now lay on it. Rest! Get a drink of soda. Ah! I am cool now. The sun is going to give me a suntan. Are you relaxed? I will go to sleep. Just relax.

Now we can take a swim! Ah! Cool, clean, water. The water feels so good. Let it get in your face. How does the water feel to you? Swim! Go under water. Then pop up. This is fun. Nice, good clean water.

The Snow of Fairyland

One cold winter night while I lie awake in bed, I heard the wind howl. Suddenly, I jumped up and ran to my window. All was still on the new fallen snow.

Then, "crash!" went a branch from a tree. Snow flew everywhere. Then my little apple tree fell with a crash. Apple blossoms flew everywhere, and the apples fell with a "thud!" A frightened look came over my face as I peered cautiously out at the lawn.

I turned away. No one was in sight. On my desk stood my dolls, Sarah and Linda. My television was standing straight and tall. I looked out again. One by one snowflakes began falling. The mean wind blew them in all directions. It looked like fairyland.

There I stood in my blue gown. How I wished I could go out and look around I thought, and I said to myself, "If I had wings, I'd fly out there with the other fairies. I would sing Christmas carols, too."

Just then I looked at my clock. It was 6 o'clock. It was morning! Just then I saw my mother. She said, "Kymberly, are you awake?" Hastily, I crawled into bed and went to sleep.

Baby Doll

Fourth Grade

On November the eleventh when we didn't have school, my father took me on a long trip. We were going to find a kitten. It would be my very own. We went to a little pet shop and bought a little kitten only four weeks old. We took her home. "She is so cute," I said.

When we reached home I was very happy. We fed her cat food and milk. While the kitten ate, I asked my mother, "What shall I name it?" My father replied, "You should name her, she's all yours." So I sat down on the floor. The kitten came and curled up on my lap. I stroked her carefully. I thought of a million names or so, but none seemed right.

Well, the cat grew and soon began to bite and meow when she was hungry. I didn't know what to call her and after a month I named her Babydoll Fee Fee Twyman.

I still have her and she is cuter. Now she bites and I say "Ouch!" but I still love her no matter what.

Kymberly Twyman

My Name is Kym

Trees and Wonderful Things

A tree is a wonderful thing.
Shiny leaves and shiny branches,
and that's not all what a tree can bring.
Pencils and paper what we get,
tables and fruit and houses, too.
But that's not all we get yet.
Chairs and shade when it's very wet,
so a tree can
keep you dry too.
Swings and baseball bats and
in the olden day, were wooden shoes!
Trees can bring a lot of
things that children like to know
and that's what the trees want to show!

Date: September 10, 1973

Charlie Brown (monologue)

Here I am, Charlie Brown, sitting alone in my room thinking over the day's happenings. Why is it I can never do anything right? For instance, my 200-word composition paper that took me all week to write was accidentally thrown in the garbage by my baby sister. I must have gone through a dozen barrels trying to find it. I found Snoopy reading it in his doghouse, laughing away as he read. Tell me, what's so funny about the life and death of Edgar Alan Poe?

Even at school, things turned out bad. Today at school, the teacher made me stand in the corner because the cute little red-head girl claimed I insulted her. What's so insulting about smiling at her?

I'll never understand why I never can do anything right, even something as simple as flying a kite. I was lucky Linus came along because he was the only one who could untangle me and the kite from the tree.

Even at the baseball game, I fouled things up and made our team look pretty bad. It all began in about the seventh inning. Our team (consisting of all the gang, including Snoopy) had two outs and it was my turn at bat. I was nervous and the bat kept slipping out of my hands.

"You can do it, Charlie Brown!" came the encouragement from Linus.

"Hit a homerun, Charlie Brown!" Lucy shouted from behind me.

The first pitch was a tricky, wind-up ball. I swung. Strike one!

I dug my fingers tighter around the bat. The second pitch was too low, but I swung anyway. Strike Two!

"Come on, Charlie Brown!" Linus was begging now.

"You better hit it, Blockhead!" Lucy growled.

The pitcher smiled mischievously at me as he prepared for the final pitch.

My Name is Kym

As the ball came towards me, I gritted my teeth and closed my eyes. Crack! I had hit the ball!

"A miracle!" I heard Lucy mutter.

"Run, Charlie Brown!" I ran with all my might. I had finally done something right! As I stood one first, I scanned the crowd in the bleachers. Yes! The cute little red-head girl was there. She had seen me hit the ball. I waved my arms, trying to get her attention. I was too busy doing this that I hadn't seen Schroeder (who was next at bat) hit the ball. I had forgotten to run to second and I found myself standing stupidly on first looking into Schroeder's angry face.

"You're out!" The umpire pointed at me. Three outs!

"You Blockhead!" Lucy was the first one to tell me how she felt. I walked to the outfield with my head down in humiliation.

The score was tied and the other team was at bat. Men were on first and third. There were two outs. Before I knew what was happening, a high fly ball came out in my direction.

"Catch it, Charlie Brown!" the team was shouting and jumping up and down. "You can do it, Charlie Brown!"

What? Was that the cute little redhead girl shouting? I stole a glance at the bleachers. Yes, it was! I blushed. The cute little red head girl had finally said something to me!

"Watch out, Charlie Brown!" The warning came too late. With a loud thud, the ball hit my head and bounced off it to the ground. The man on third scored and the other team won the game.

"You blockhead, Charlie Brown!" My team shouted at me angrily as they walked by. "You are and always will be a blockhead, Charlie Brown!"

I really felt bad. How could I ever face the team again? Even my own dog has turned against me.

Well, that was how my day went. I lived one nightmare after another. It's getting late now and its almost time for bed. That was one unpredictable day with Charlie Brown. Tune in tomorrow for another.

Kym
the
Poet

Love Is

Peabody High School
12th Grade (circa 1976)

Love is unique. Two shadows in the park.

Loving is beautiful. A warm, satisfying feeling.

Love is profound. Remembering and understanding

the experience.

Love.   I love the word!

I love that feeling!

I love . . . You.

Appraisal

The antennas are strangling me, puncturing my mind.
Criminal! Corrupting the innocent, oh shame!
I've become lost in a fog of distorted images—
a shattered victim of yesterday's world—
simplicity and love, as natural as the wind.
Come forth and blow away the poisoning fog.
Yet, as it lifts, I no longer recognize the screen.
Cover my eyes! I can't bear to look!
The fog has left a hardened tar upon the screen,
black with violence, hate, and death. Ugh!
Are we to live in a clouded world forever?
TV, look at tomorrow's children. Oh, please look!

See what you've done . . . what you're doing.

A stronger wind will have to blow away
that suffocating fog

before we die of pot-holed minds.

My Name is Kym

A Reflection

Eternal pain and bittersweet agony behind a painted smile . . .
I sense the sharp vibrations in your
FACE.

Silent hatred and short-lived sorrow . . .
These are the unspoken words upon your
LIPS.

Crushed memories of decades gone by . . .
Dark pools of brown captured it all
EYES.

I cannot quietly gaze into your face . . .
My intimate feelings and troubled thoughts are far too
DEEP.

I cannot transmit words to your cracked, dry lips . . .
It is a message of stinging
REVENGE.

I cannot pretend, for eyes do not lie . . .
My cold, insolent stares melt to
WATER.

I cannot concentrate; my delicate feelings are shattered . . .
Yes, it is you who possesses the
POWER.

Victory is won, and you are content . . .
Chastise my innocence, criticize my
WEAKNESS.

I wretchedly weep for myself and for you . . .
The suffocating air rings loudly with your
LAUGHTER.

. . . What kind of person am I?
ARE WE?
For I am you . . . and . . . you are me.
YET WE ARE VERY DIFFERENT.

Boring Beginnings with Worn-Out Endings

The final day of a final month—a fading period of a year
    that accumulated memories
        and plucked them high into the air
        with a single gold tooth.

Today—a night of dire confusion.
    The tender beginnings of a new, expectant love,
        yet I do not know how to handle it
          —NOT ANY MORE—

The branch was abruptly broken off of a past love,
    but the sibling bud, withered and beaten down
    desperately struggles to bloom;
        and I don't understand my mixed emotions
          —NOT ANYMORE—

The wished upon star never twinkled its greeting in return,
      and so I must turn toward a distant horizon.
      Yet the temptation to look around
      is so intense, so unmistakably urgent
          that I no longer can control it
            ——NOT ANYMORE——

What am I to say, as the young hand-me-down——
      the victim of a bitter game
      in which the current winner is full of evil plans
      that never fail to trap and deceive?

Where am I to run, in a forest
      too thick to crawl,
      too cloudy to scan,
      the befriended horizon for a glimpse
      of a forgotten rainbow?

My Name is Kym

Kym at 15 years of age

Death Trap

The spider's victim . . .
She desperately clings to its imperfect web.
Death dances tauntingly above her sweat-beaded brow,
taunting and teasing as she moaned in despair.

Life coos patiently at her shoulder;
it's all a matter of time.
Her tear-streaked almond eyes are closed.
The pepper-salt hair lies in a tangled heap
about the cold, limp pillow.

Pale, shapeless lips curl distinctly in a frown—
a wince as the pain from her heaving chest
shatters throughout the decaying body.
visions, nightmares . . . a stifled scream . . .
an endless roller-coaster ride—

Too many curves and no seatbelts,
and then . . . and then a sigh of inner peace
escapes from quivering lips.

Death is laughing now. Can't you hear?
The haughty spider is moving down the web . . .
I took her clammy hand and squeezed it
gently . . .

"Hang on to your web," I whispered,
As the bittersweet tears streamed down
my anguished face,
"Hang on to the delicate threads of Life!"

My Name is Kym

Destination

She desperately captures the moment—clinging to uncommon fears
and bearing the wrath of her ridiculed race.

She furiously captures the moment—bittersweet afflictions
have marred her mind and driven her insane.

(Where were you when she cried out in pain?)

She modestly captures the moment—curved, agile fingers
poised defiantly on her bare hips.

She naively captures the moment—stripped of Life's gold threads
and the silver strings of Truth.

(Where were you in her tortured youth?)

She proudly captures the moment—the radiance of an ageless face
and unspoken words glow in the dawn.

She vibrantly captures the moment—a distorted maze
of colorful emotions darkens her face and slurs her speech.

(Where were you as the quiet innocence
drained from her body—a victim of the leech?)

She captures the moment with one hesitant smile
that reveals her personal beauty
and creates a unique
expression of . . .

WOMANHOOD.

Disappointment

I'm lost in the sea of confusion,
content to grope around in the darkness
of a thousand unanswered questions.
Drowning in a whirlpool of memories;
satisfaction achieved through ignorance,
remaining at the starting block,
afraid to race against my shadow
for fear it may win and I will be
forever trapped in the web
of my own unfulfilled desires.

Freestyle

"Letting go
Swaying in a distant breeze
Reaching out
Feeling mellow on a natural high
Soaring upward
Chasing rainbows with a smile
Being me . . ."

Wondering where our smiles decide to go
When they have been there so long
In a time and place we once knew
And created with a patience so still
There was no love that could describe
The words never spoken with lips
Molded into a familiar shape
A smile . . . It is all we have now.

Frenzy

I'm in a hurry . . .
coasting, gliding,
tumbling, propelling,
accelerating beyond all speed limitations.

I'm ready to depart,
prepared to take a solitary flight
and flee from that other hurricane
into a timeless dark space
that is lighted by
a glow of inner joy.

Lost Love

Peabody High School
12th grade (circa 1976)

Our love is an old worn page, turned too many times—
shriveled in the heat of anger.

Shredded for scandalous lust,
and discarded by bitter jealousy.

Strike a match if you dare and destroy memories.

Let a disintegrating heart scatter like ashes
in the wind,
darkening the sun littering the sky
with my loss.

I refuse to cry; regret is for the weak.

A howling wind sprinkles the sodden soot upon my doorstep.

"Leave me alone," I cry out in pain.

I shiver in the dying wind as I take the broom
to sweep up memories

And throw

      my life

          away . . .

Kymberly Twyman McEnheimer

My Dogs

November 13, 1976

After four dogs (Peppy, Spot, Terry, Sheba) plus 12 roly-poly puppies, 2 cats and 20 kittens (Baby Doll, Toby, Misty, etc., etc.) 4 turtles, 25 tropical fish, 1 snail, and a sprinkle of babies, 3 goldfish, 1 hamster affectionately named Cho-Cho. Whew (pant, pant, sigh). Now there's Jaiamie a loveable mischievous, adventurous, bow-legged, flea-bitten, spoiled toy poodle. Oh well . . . this may very well be, er change that: This is the start of another long run of future, four-legged Twymans. I can't imagine what's next. Kym loves her animals.

M.M.

Mellow is melodic magic . . .

it's a matter of subsiding, declining,

and submerging into a rhythmic feeling,

very deeply . . . very slowly . . .

Quietly sinking into warm, sensuous folds of luxury;

never wanting to emerge again.

That's mystic . . . It is dusting the silver bottom,

caressing the golden sides

with the last bronze rag she possesses.

Mellow is feeling drained;

completely hollow inside and vibrating with the echoes.

Desperately desiring passion's pleasures to sneak

within and make life full again——Raw Love.

Now, that's magic . . . it's tingling all over——

warm and soft, gentle and so tender

that the body is sensitive to touch

and can't stand gentle pain.

To feel melodic is to have created the musical score

and sing the soothing song alone.

She has tumbled through a personal hurricane

in order to sense the satisfaction.

H-m-m-m . . . She is ready for mellow . . . Are you?

Kymberly Twyman McEnheimer

Places

Places are demon cases—draining earned money

    from souvenir parasites on sweltering, tropical islands.

Places are priceless vases—well-remembered treasures

    teetering on the edge of Life's grand piano.

Places are hastily said graces—stop-and-go chaos

    that leaves little time for true appreciation.

Places are knotted shoelaces—crowded highways, roadblocks,

    and congested traffic jams leading nowhere.

Places are stolen bases—a dash to first and a quick slide

    to third; there's no place like home.

Places are expressionless faces—gray wrinkles

    and dry toothless smiles haunting dusty ghost towns.

Places are slow paces—made by green mother turtles

    window-shopping with tired children in emerald cities.

Places are decayed spaces—reproduced, reconstructed,

    and remodeled to be admired as "new."

Places are futile races—a confused mob of tourists,

    anxious to see blank walls of scenery.

Places are . . .

    tearful faces of lost lovers

in monotonous races,

    stealing heart-shaped bases

on spotted spaces.

My Name is Kym

Remembering

The second after yesterday
is a time of need, a desire to live.

Striving for the star that shirks from touch,
fulfilling the dream that lacks time to create.

It becomes an hour that realized its destiny,
yet wanders past the sixty-second count
because it is unique,

Fearlessly alone and sometimes forgotten.

I will not deny it, nor betray its company.

For that second is a reflection of myself,
although I have always existed
in tomorrow's third shadow.

Revelation

It was a journey to nowhere
I took a dizzy ride with them.

They laughed, spinning endlessly on
the merry-go-round that mocks
the time and future.

Embedded in the middle, I felt trapped
in the sweet, burning stickiness
of their tempting honey.

They loved its taste,
craving for more and convulsing in delight
while the child's ride moaned a bittersweet ballad.

I was violently spun off from whirling nonsense,
propelling into empty space,
nauseated, disgusted . . . sick with fear.

Yet, I picked myself up,
turning to gaze cautiously around in wonder,
realizing the luck, guarding the shock—

I am free!

The Champion

Evil bears the face of enchantment,
    shameless intensity,
        a naked lust.

Evil possesses the expression of innocence,
    the quietness of satisfaction,
        the eyes of blazing desire.

Evil moans the voice of ecstasy,
    whispers with deceit,
        cries with passion.

Evil is the champion of Evil.
    The starry-eyed followers
        trudge along the sunbaked road;
    the clatter of loose screws
        In hollow heads.

My distinct sound: *silence*
    is not heard among them . . .

Kymberly Twyman McEnheimer

The Outsider

I am alien to love.
I recognize its beauty at a distance,
     yet it is not appreciated by my scornful eyes.

I comprehend its treasure,
     yet I do not seek the prize, for it is not rightfully mine
          to obtain.

I am a stranger to the lust of passionate desires.

I view its absurdity with a critical scorn,
     a bitter laugh that echoes across
          the plains of my distorted mind.

I am invisible,
     no longer existing
          within the boundaries of the heart.

The Church

Twinkling, yet faded brown eyes;
    pale shallow cheeks and a crooked, toothless smile.
Warm crushing handshakes;
    a quickly whispered greeting.

Chipped black canes clatter against the wooden benches
    as elderly remnants of a past era hobble to their seats
        with solemn and worn—almost grim—expressions.

Familiar faces from home and abroad
    meet my dewy eyes
        as I silently gaze about.

Dimly-lit chandeliers droop monstrously
    from an arched ceiling.

Archaic stained-glass windows
    depict a story of an ancient man
        who brought the gift of Love.

The heavy drone of a distant organ;
    the rustling of many choir robes.

A beautiful hymn; the fluent blend of voices
      causes my heart to flutter with joy.

Words: a message in song floats
      across the room, across the street.

Perhaps it will touch a dark stranger
      from a desolate home, a musty bar.

         (We cannot conceal the rebirth of the hour.)

A final hymn, a sweet hour of prayer.
The message is clear; I have been cleansed.

         (We cannot conceal the rebirth of the hour)

The spirit follows us out into the drizzling rain,
      the heavy gray clouds.

      It clings;

         it is ours forever.

We have learned . . .

         now we must apply.

The Purse

Creased leather and frayed lining

Stray bobby pins, crumpled tissue, a diary

Pencils, pens, lost coins, buckles

Wrappers, wallets, water stains

An empty lipstick tube, comb and brush

Little notes

Zippered in darkness.

The Stabbing

Pain expressed in a thousand words,
    a vibrating sensation teetering
        on the brink of instability.

A feeling incapable of expression
    for it refuses understanding
        and relishes confusion.

The delights of perplexity—
    a mind in chaos,

Yet, this legitimate pain
            is graceless and sincere.

The Visit

The song of the nightingales . . .
echoing through the paint-chipped walls,
scurrying along the zig-zagged cracks that decorate the ceiling.

A harmonious tune floats across the dusty old furniture,
rolls along the uneven, rugless floor.

A message of love burrows gently in the folds of soft bosoms,
nestling deeper into the rekindled warmth
of weak hearts.

The song of the nightingales . . .
dulled hearing—faded eyesight—dry, cracked throats—
arthritic hands—
strained to hum along or tap a calloused foot in beat,
as we sang . . . as we sang carols of Love.
as I swelled . . . as I swelled with Pride.

I felt an inner tranquility . . . I felt that I had touched
(A heart)—(a soul)—(a mind)
The song of the nightingales . . .

They listened from their hospital beds
and from their creaking rocking chairs,
I wanted desperately to cry out with joy . . .
I wanted anxiously to share my ecstasy.

As a crooked smile

Upon the beaming, decaying face

Sought my eyes

And held it there.

Kymberly Twyman McEnheimer

#

Time is bitter and stretches on . . .

Time does not wait for the innocent victim
      to squeeze it within his grasp
      in search of physical truth.

Time sifts, like trivial particles of sand,
      through rough calloused hands,
      and rides with the laughing wind.

Time will not let the heart-broke woman,
      who weeps by the ashes,
      caress the sweet memories created for her.

Time is bitter and stretches on . . .

Time shrivels and curls like fallen dead leaves
      in the grass,
      leaving angry wrinkles on a grandmother's face.

Time refuses to wait for maturity,
      as the wriggling, new-born baby
      lies helplessly on the Bank of Life.

Time leaves scars, as it flings invisible arrows
      of pain and sorrow,
      destroying the heart and mind.

Time devours freedom,
      for there is no quiet hollow in which to escape
      and discover a true identity.

Time will scorn the clock that ticks away
      the precious hours spent in relaxation.

Time does not need or desire the friendship
      of the ragged stranger haunting the dusty roads.

Time does not care, for time is . . .
              bitter and . . .
                  stretches on . . .

                          My Name is Kym

To Be Is To Be

What does it feel like to be?

I'm experiencing it now.

Being is very personal—that which expresses me.

My thoughts

And conflictions;

My inner emotions

Cling to the languid body, fearful to let go.

I can softly whisper, "I am; this is me;

My feelings are."

A perfected circle revolves around my individuality,

Giving me the power to close out a patterned world,

Forming my own Uniqueness.

I've been given names that invade my identity:

"A human being, a homo-sapiens, a woman."

Bursting free from all constricting bonds,

I form a class of my own.

Turn to gaze respectfully at me, world—

I am here, uninhibited,

And there, unlimited—yet,

very much

alone.

Kymberly Twyman McEnheimer

Two in a Shadow for One

What shall become of the withdrawn child
who huddles behind her transparent cloud
      In the corner of reality?

Where will she go?

What may she seek

What can she grasp
          to call her own unique identity?

The answer lies behind my blinded eyes.

All is dark and no one can see it,
         not even her.

She will trudge on,
      fleeing from the forbidden touch
         of yesterday's past.

She shuns its warmth . . . I weep from its chill.

All About Kym

Discover Me

I want to discover myself, my true identity and find out who I really am. For fourteen years I have lived and say honestly I don't know myself. What am I like through someone else's eyes? What am I like through my own eyes?

I look in the mirror and see a small lonely girl staring back defensively. I stare in that mirror for hours trying to see deeper inside, but I only see a pair of large owl-like eyes staring innocently back. I want to be my own self and have some own pattern that is truly mine and no one else's.

I remember when I was younger and truly fascinated by princesses, queens, the whole bit. I tried to copy their roles and be like them. But this is a real world where there aren't such things. I'm living in a black ghetto where life is real and hard.

A few years back when I first began my writing, I wrote about things that I have read to be true, but were not. Such as girls wondering about dates. Shy, unpopular girls who worried. The really goody-goody type. But now as I grow older and have decided to write even more, I am changing that kind of pattern. I must write about the things that are real to me, not what is not.

My life and the life today are not as those kinds of books say. Yes, I was really sucked in with all that kind of thing and imagined that I would be going to little dances and fussing with my hair and all that kind of jive. I'm not saying that all of that kind of thing is gone, it's still happening, but let's face it. I live in a black neighborhood where my date doesn't take me to the neighborhood ice-skating rink, or we take a swim in the lake down the road.

Maybe all that I am saying is really not making sense. Maybe I won't be a writer after all. I'm really quite mixed up. But I know I won't write very many if none at all kind of stories that I was brought up on. I will write what is real to me, the real thing. How life is today. I don't want young people to read my writings some day and follow that pattern that I did. I want them to understand the full meaning of life, the deep-down hard facts. How life really is so that they will be able to

My Name is Kym

face it with strength and courage and will be prepared to challenge the unexpected. Don't accept life for what it is. Don't sit back and let others do everything. Step up in the front and speak what you feel. I'm not much on expressing my feelings orally, but I will try to express my words, thoughts, and actions through my writing.

My Life

I was born on a sunny Wednesday, June 17, 1959, in West Penn Hospital. My parents, Juanita and Gerald, were very proud. They had only been married two years (1957) when I was born. Had I only been born one year before, my grandfather, Jesse Bagley (mother's side) could have seen me. He died in February of '58. My grandmother, Celia, told me quite a lot of his life when I was small and made him seem like such a fascinating person. I wished I had been living in that time to really know him. My other grandfather on my father's side (Twyman) died many years before and I wasn't told much about him by my father or my grandmother, Ruth.

I am the only child, but I had always wished to have a brother or a sister, in fact as many as my parents could handle, which wasn't much on Dad's part. He often was grumpy and once my mother told me, he wasn't all that crazy about kids. In my younger years, brothers and sisters didn't matter so much, since my mother and father always bought me toys and games and I supposed another addition to the family might interfere.

Of course in one way or another, I found out what it's like to have other kids around. I had so many cousins that even as I got older, I still didn't know all of them. When I was small, I had cousins come over and spend the night. Mostly it was my cousin, Sheryl, who was a year older and my cousin, Chrissy, who was two years younger. Chrissy and I were the closest of cousins and sometimes people called us sisters since there is a resemblance. Chrissy came from a large family of seven children (five boys and two girls). Her older sister, Sandy, was in college and stayed with me to get away sometimes from her brothers. The large Bell family was related to our family on both sides. As we grew older and I was gradually becoming a teen-ager, Chrissy and I grew slightly apart. As for me and my cousin, Sheryl, we grew apart at about the time she was eleven and I was nine. Sheryl and her family moved from our neighborhood, Homewood, to Garfield which was farther, and we had less contact except for the visits me and my family made as often as we could.

My Name is Kym

I attended nursery school at Bethesda Church when I was four years old. My grandmother, Celia, whom I call Nana, took me down to the church every morning around ten o'clock and picked me up at about three. I was very small and quite shy which followed me through a third of my life. But despite this, I made a few friends one of whom I stayed friends with a great deal of my life. The little girl's name was Donna and her long dark-brown braids fascinated me. I mean, I had hair almost as long as she had, but there was something about her that interested me. She was my size if not a tiny bit bigger and was also quite shy. Unlike me, she had a big brother named Phillip whom her family called Skipper. She often talked about her big brother who at the time was about a senior in high school. I was jealous because I too wanted a big brother.

Donna and I started out slow, but soon enough we became good friends. I found out that we both went to the same church, (St. James AME), and that our parents were casual acquaintances. Soon my grandmother began walking us both home from Bethesda and sometimes Donna's or my father would drive us home. Donna and I had common interests when we were small. I for one had a large collection of dolls like most little girls around my age. Donna had several too and soon we began visiting to play together. My mother felt this was good for me, since I stayed home a great deal playing by myself. Even though I had fun over at Donna's house, it seemed I always felt the best security at home. I guess this resulted from being the only child.

I started kindergarten at Belmar Elementary School shortly after I turned five years old. Donna and I were in the same room and this made us very happy. At those early times she was what I called a security blanket besides my mother and father, and I'm sure it was likewise. I also met a new friend named Michelle, who moved about four houses down from me. Michelle was not an only child either but had three brothers. I didn't mind for Michelle and I became fast friends also. She was also in my room at kindergarten and there we talked and played together as well as after school. My grandmother still took me to school and Michelle was included.

The school, which I attended until I graduated in sixth grade, seemed very large to me in those days. There were many kids and we had to be careful not to get knocked down by the older ones. Donna lived right across the street from Belmar while Michelle and I lived several blocks away. Really it wasn't far since I walked the very same route for a great many years.

In kindergarten we had a very mean teacher by the name of Miss Sullivan. She was very large and was slightly prejudiced in our all-black school. Her huge body towered over us small kindergarteners and everyone in the class was kind of afraid of her.

In kindergarten we mostly sat on the floor which made my dresses become dirty and soiled. It was a rare time we sat at the tables even though there was a large set. I don't remember much during my year in kindergarten except that we played many games, fingerpainted, sang along as Miss Sullivan played her large brown piano, worked with clay, listened to stories, and drank our daily milk and cookies at lunchtime. In the kindergarten program there were two shifts. The morning session from 8:30 to 11:25 and the afternoon session from 12:30 to 3:25.

I remember the days before I started school around early September, I received a letter from the school accepting me into kindergarten and the shift that I was assigned to. It turned out to be the morning session which prepared me for getting up early for school in the years to follow. My mother and father were proud as they often were in certain things that I did. Shouldn't every parent?

No Hope to Spare

I am a forgotten alien, surrounded by the hostile walls

of a bitter reality.

I can no longer depict my precious dreams,

for they have been singed at the tender roots

of their sporadic being.

Hope remains in the dark corner of my tortured mind;

I have not closed my eyes to the nakedness

of empty feelings.

I have not drawn the transparent curtains

on the blinding ignorance

of the light of lust.

I have not turned my heart from those who abuse

the sacred throne of love,

wallowing like gluttonous pigs at its base.

I have tried to be myself,

yet no one recognizes the stranger

I shall always be—

sometimes . . . not even me.

Kymberly Twyman McEnheimer

Reflections Upon Viewing a Famous Poet

I could sympathize, somehow relate to the struggle,
Yet as an observer, a misfit in time.
I sensed the gripping reality
Vibrated with the harsh tones of bitterness
And the melodic thrust of an imbedded pain.
Moments that demanded laughter,
Seconds reliving a past only read in fairy tales.
Opportunities to grasp the sensuous feeling
Without fleeing from the threat of being black.
Hard times, warm memories, ecstatic recollections.
A hoarse voice that spoke for us all,
But does it really?
Wondering about the afterthought,
puzzled by a sensation unknown and misunderstood,
desiring to belong with a pattern of life—
yet we all create different molds
melted into one creation of truth.

My Name is Kym

Kym's High School Graduation Picture

Kym
Coming
of
Age

Love Flows In . . .

May 1, 1977

Love flows in quick ecstasies, rapid movements, flustering fantasies and prolonged excursions . . .

Love arrives in the heat of the night, at the crack of dawn and on the dog day afternoon . . .

Love is the lonely one, free and single that experiences the passion and remembers the pain . . .

Love has faith in those who desire to be needed by someone special, for hate is always on its heels . . .

Love is always there, picking up headache's scattered pieces and . . . moving on . . .

a sisterhood of women with common interests and
goals to live and work together and enjoy close friendships.

Merry-Go-Round Earth

Advanced Composition Period 6
April 4, 1977 (age 18) – Mrs. Givan

"Alcohol and drug abuse have been overwhelmingly irrelevant,
entirely absurd!
Food prices are obviously insane,
indubitably inequitable!
Increasing divorce rates are simply baffling,
literally incomprehensible!
Pollution is solely disserviceable,
universally nauseating!
Pornographic movies are usually abhorrent,
horribly sinister!
Poverty in America is unmistakably inexcusable,
totally senseless!
Rebellious teenagers are unquestionably incompetent,
extremely obnoxious!
Young marriage is purely irrational,
truly unjustifiable!
I don't dare predict where
this unbalanced merry-go-round called Earth
is teetering to!
Oh, how dreadful! My dizzy life
has become extremely disturbing, absolutely revolting,
and indisputably ironical for . . .

Teddy Bear and I to bear!"

My Name is Kym

Free

Advanced Composition Period 6
February 14, 1977 (age 17) — Mrs. Givan

Free

Free has caused bitter headaches for which endless days
I've cried
Free left me broken, despaired and wishing I could have
died.
Free is an ageless question——pondered, puzzled
and tried.
Free has opened closed eyes——realizing after years of
trust, he's lied.
Free is gazing out a rain-streaked window counting how
often I've sighed.
Free has picked me up, pushed me around——the sore
bumper of the ride.
Free is running here, going there, searching for an
uncrowded shadow to hide.
Free laps at my swollen feet as it kisses the shore,
then dashes away, rejoining the tide.
Free can be measured, for it's seven hearts long and seven hearts
wide.
Free is a delicate law——signed, sealed, and delivered to abide.
Free is us, ours, and we——mutual stars that never collide.
Free has helped mend shattered pieces——an everlasting guide.
Free will help me to say to you as I humbly confide:
Free wants your friendship, full of love and never denied.

Hyperboles

Advanced Composition Period 6
Due: May 13, 1977 (age 17) — Mrs. Givan

1. Our billowed dreams float across the threatening skies in search of a thunderstorm.

2. The frivolous pains of hunger played hopscotch across my stomach.

3. Our love dribbled across the floor and clashed against the rim of rejection before it bounced away.

4. He sprained his ankle a thousand times before he felt the pain of lost love.

5. Despite their persistent hospitality, I was reluctant to dance with the jovial ghosts at the house party.

6. The U.S. embraces Russia and cries on its stiff shoulder for friendship.

7. The whimpering cries of the drowning dog continuously echo through the trees above the pond.

8. Her hair was as black as the eclipse that rose in her eyes.

9. The girl's humiliation bore heavily on her thin shoulders as she sank in the quicksand of guilt.

10. She transformed into a polka-dotted silver dollar and he into an overdone pancake as he rolled off the train.

My Name is Kym

Is There Freedom?

Peabody High School
Pittsburgh, Pa. 15206
Age: 17 (senior)

Sitting . . . sitting and sighing, waiting on an inspiration.

Freedom . . . I can't see you.

The beautiful rainbow of hope that graced the sky of our forefathers has died in the eyes of yesterday's youth. The sacred memories recreated by proud, black grandmothers have been marred by a new, careless generation. The growth of our youth—our tall, dark children of tomorrow—has been stunted by a mental and physical abuse. We reach toward the sky and find that our stars—the stars that led Harriet Tubman to freedom—are gone. The sun that bore its fervent rays upon the weary backs of humble cotton-pickers no longer supplies the warmth of love; the moon that received the deep, powerful spirituals from lonely slave quarters has shunned the night. The youth of today grope blindly about in a dark and hostile world in search of a remnant of an era too painful to remember for many. The silent, gaunt man who slumps in a nearby armchair dimly reviews the past as an old worn page turned too many times for emphasis, repetition, and clarification. Rocking slightly, he folds and unfolds his gnarled black hands as an incoherent hymn softly escapes from thick, shapeless lips.

Freedom . . . I can't hear you.

> '*Kum Ba Yah, my Lord,*
> *Kum Ba Yah.*
> *Someone's praying, Lord,*
> *Kum Ba Yah . . .*'

A child kneels beside a tattered bed with his dirty and sticky hands clasped tightly in prayer. His naked back is marred by numerus welts

Kymberly Twyman McEnheimer

and a dull moonlight boldly reveals bruises on the tiny, tear-stained face. Who is to blame? Who took the time to understand? Father stumbles clumsily from the neon-lit bar and lies shamelessly in the gutter. The nauseating stench of hopelessness wafts across the city and hovers tauntingly like a dark shadow above the praying child's head. The dark lady of the night—a troubled mother returns to her home with unwanted guests of inner frustrations that torment the whimpering child.

Freedom, can you hear the stabbing cries of a beaten little boy? Open your ears and listen . . .

Freedom——I can hear you!
The clank of chain gangs stalking the dusty roads on starry nights.

Freedom——I can see you!
Cotton fields and bus boycotts; the bitter agony upon the faces of my Negro brothers.

Freedom——I can taste you!
The salty tears of imagined pain; an undying struggle as we sank in the quicksand of slavery.

Freedom——I-I-I can't feel you
. . . (not yet) . . .

I'm waiting on my inspiration.
I want to feel the solid black pride felt by
my forefathers swell within me.
I want to feel the warmth of a beautiful heritage
as I lift my beaming black face toward the sky.
I want to feel the firm embrace of my proud dark grandmother.

I want to feel the swirling current take me up as I begin my journey to—
Freedom
. . . I need you,
my tall black brothers and sisters need you.

My Name is Kym

Advice and My Evaluation of Advanced Composition

Advanced composition is a true example that the impossible can be accomplished. There are very few easy streets, but a series of dark, back roads. It takes continuous hard work to achieve a satisfying goal and stand in the light on the paved road of success. One has to feel pride of becoming a better writer. It begins at the feet and slowly works its way up. When the proud student leaves the class at the end of the year, his steps are light, and his head is held high. It is a beautiful experience that I hope other students will share.

The skills acquired and strengthened during the year will prove to be very useful in the future as well as everyday life. How well one writes determines the person in the eyes of others. I reflected upon each journal entry as an experience or adventure that was climaxed when shared with the class during the Monday writings. The journals were an excellent way to express inner feelings that ordinarily would not have emerged.

Think carefully as you write the weekly papers. It takes time and self-patience in order to turn in a paper that speaks for you. Everyone is not a natural writer and the right words will not always seemingly "appear" to jot down. A good student must realize his own weaknesses, because one must have a good attitude towards writing. We all have our dry periods in which sentences seem to become tangled before our eyes and the wrong words run off the page. I believe that this is the true test of a writer.

Don't give up! Have confidence in yourself and this familiar symptom will clear up. Writing is not a comical game and it should always be handled seriously. Mrs. Givan enforces this rule but be smart and know what is expected ahead of time. The dedicated writer gives

Kymberly Twyman McEnheimer

deep thought to every single word on the page. Be careful of punctuation. Words are like people. They do not like to be misspelled or abused by careless errors. An "A" on a paper should create a smile and a sigh of relief. Do not get lazy or take writing for granted if this grade becomes a familiar sight. This is the worst way to handle writing because the grade will soon become quite rare if a student slackens.

I consider myself a devoted student of Mrs. Givan. The class could have existed forever, because she gave me the added encouragement to write as well as I could. This is very important in creative writing because it involves feelings and a sharp disapproval, for a rejection can hurt mentally. I believe that a writer needs someone's approval now and then in order to develop his work naturally. I hope to become a famous author of poems, short stories, novels, etc., and I can honestly say that I'll always remember my advanced composition teacher in high school. I learned how to express in a much more intimate way. Often I was shocked after proofreading a paper at how little I knew about myself. I honestly didn't realize my own inner feelings. It was like reading a stranger's poem and yet I could relate to it. For it was a part of me that I never knew before. Mrs. Givan has helped me in more ways than she or I could imagine. I hope that she will continue to offer her unselfish and rewarding services to the upcoming years' students with pen and paper in hand, eager to express, create and emerge successful.

Wearing the Pin of

A
K
A

The proud and patient
all wear the pin of Alpha Kappa Alpha
with heads held high in reverence and respect
bearing the precious name within
their hearts.

To wear the sacred pin bearing the
respected name of Alpha Kappa Alpha
becomes a symbol of pride, dedication
and promise,
of wishes granted and heads bowed
humbly in unity.

The pin of Alpha Kappa Alpha
is a symbol of unity, sisterhood,
and deep-rooted pride—
a precious gift forever to be
treasured.
And never to be rejected,
forgotten, or denied.

Alpha Kappa Alpha

Kym graduated from Duquesne University

When going through Kym's papers, I found this letter she wrote in 1981 to a potential employer. I thought it summarized her own perspective on her writing skills. – Juanita

Dear Personnel Manager,

I would like to be considered for a creative or technical writing position with your company. I am a May 1981 graduate of Duquesne University with a Bachelor of Arts degree in English. I had a double minor in psychology and social communications.

My writing experiences include the publication of several short stories and poems. These works have received recognition in *The Duquesne University Magazine*, *The Eye*, a quarterly publication of the Carnegie Library of Pittsburgh, and *Young America Sings*, an annual anthology of poems by high school students sponsored by The National Poetry Press.

I feel my courses in Technical and Professional Writing and Writing for Business and Industry have improved my skills in a formerly unknown area. I excelled with study and practice. Both courses were devoted to the principles and styles of efficient technical writing. I learned how to transform complex material into concise and coherent language for the average reader. There was a great deal of emphasis placed upon the definitions and descriptions of mechanisms and processes. Other course highlights included writing proposals, and progress and recommendation reports.

My working experiences do not directly reflect my writing abilities. These experiences have usually been summer employment because of my academic studies. However, I feel qualified for a creative or technical writing position based on my previous and present writing experiences within and outside of the university curriculum. Please feel free to contact me. Thank you very much.

Kymberly S. Twyman
June 11, 1981

Kym

and

Family

My Aunt Ruth Twyman Bell
(1929 -1976)

DEAR GOD, WHY?

Oh God, why take a life so precious?
Oh God, why take a vivid memory an enchanted dream, a beautiful kaleidoscope?
There must be a reason
Oh, God, I loved a warm, vibrant person

— A woman — a mother

The loss of a mother, one of the most precious gifts that life has to offer.

Oh Lord, to take her away and leave 7 desolate children and a strong faithful husband.

I feel so lucky. I mean I have a mother and yet they don't. Oh God, I look at Pumpkin and I think, "I was 7 years old, I had a mother to watch over me . . . why couldn't her . . . ?"

Oh dear God, why must they be deprived?

I love my mother and if anything should happen to her, yet I feel Chrissy's loss just as badly.

To grow up without her voice, her smile, her loving care.

Their home will forever hold an empty place at the table, in the kitchen in their . . . hearts.

I'm praying for every single one of them.

God bless, dear Uncle Paul, and Sandy and Paul II and Chrissy and John and Kevin and Kelly and help little Pumpkin little Gerald. And God, help my father, a devoted brother, and Uncle Buddy the oldest and also God take care of Aunt Lil who has lost a beautiful sister.

She is resting in peace, where there's no more pain to suffer through . . . She is sitting beside You and her sweet mother, Ruth, my dear grandmother.

I can look toward the sky and see them, Lord . . .

They are calm now, Lord . . . Thank You.

My Name is Kym

Aunt Ruth's Children

Family Reunion

July 2, 1977

Twenty years from now it won't matter what color outfit I wore or whether or not I walked around barefoot all afternoon. It won't matter what cousins argued among each other at the card table or ate together around the barbeque grills. Time will have changed the feelings of mixed emotions — seeing old faces for a second or third time around or chattering easily with the familiar city relatives while anxiously but cautiously desiring to become acquainted with new faces.

I can never forget the starry look in Nana's eyes as she made the first speech around the graduate's table, honoring myself, Dale, Walter, and Kenny. She spoke softly in her usual hoarse voice that has become a part of her over the past year. She spoke of pride and an unmatched happiness I could see the Bells — Alonzo and Cora smiling down from heaven's glory. M-M-M Greatgrandpa and Grandma I could see Aunt Ruth's smile too at the heavenly gates quietly watching us all and wishing the best for her children. I can never forget these beautiful relatives. I can never relive such wonderful moments. Yet will the little children of today remember and treasure the gift, yes, the gift, that our family has been blessed with? It's such a glorious feeling.

It's been such a lovely day. I'll always remember the very first reunion. I'll always remember our special gift of love.

Bell Family Reunion — Washington D.C.

✶✶✶✶✶

Kym was an only child but she loved her cousins who were an important part of her life. Here is a list of all her first cousins in their order of age and include some from Alabama (my side of the family) and Pittsburgh (my husband's side of the family). - Juanita

Theresa Bagley Davis
Robert Twyman (Bobby)
Winfred Bagley (Winne)
Robert Henderson (Sonny)
Cassandra Brown (Sandy)
Leslie Buckley
Walter Twyman (Little Buddy)
Paul Bell III
Nathaniel Bagley
Hershel Bagley Jr. (Buddy)
D. Christine Bell (Chris)
M. Shawn Bagley
Judieth Bagley (Judy)
John Bell
Adrian Bagley (Dana)
Robin Bagley
Kevin Bell (twins)
Kelly Bell (twins)
Priscilla Bagley
Jeffrey Bagley
Gerald Bell (Pumpkin)
Natalyn Bagley Carter
Sheryl Pinson

My Name is Kym

A Tribute to a Quiet Father

Can perfection truly be found in a father's love?
Can every living thing stop breathing and stare in awe at a father's smile?
Can the world end its constant battle with human life and behold the rare
wonder of a father's voice?
It can be done . . .
It will be done . . .
It has been done . . . in our dreams.
A father's special gift with words echoes through our minds with
meaningful advice, highly regarded and respected,
FOR THERE WILL NEVER BE ANOTHER LIKE HIM.
A silent stranger cannot replace the familiar expression of a father's
eyes—deep with pride and moist with affection.
An unknown man cannot invade the warm, invisible circle created by
a father as he quietly embraces his loving children.
FOR THERE WILL NEVER BE ANOTHER LIKE HIM.
The flawless gentleman who creates sacred memories for me, for you
will always be there—
to hold a trembling hand—when you need him.
to dry ceaseless tears—when you need him.
to embrace a seemingly endless pain and
comfort—when you need him.
to counsel and protect—when you need him.
A father's mental strength can overpower the threatening odds,
and stand triumphantly on the winning side of Love.

Open your folded arms and embrace and cherish his undying affection.
Open your tightly closed eyes and realize his unique and natural goodness.
Open your beating heart and allow melodic vibrations to flow forth.
Open your entire self and pay a pure and simple tribute to
a beautiful man who is mine
is yours
Always,
for he is like a precious rose forever in bloom.

Kymberly Twyman McEnheimer   81

Kym with her mother, father, and two young sons

Mom

When I think about my mother, no words can truly express all that she means to me. She is a symbol of faith, hope, love, and pride. My mother is like a rare pearl, outshining all others because I love and respect her dearly. She has been, and will always be, an inspiration in my life because she has always been there when I needed her, offering support and guidance. She never fails to speak her mind in any situation, yet her quiet criticism is really a wisdom to be admired.

She unselfishly gives of herself to everyone she encounters— willing and able to help with kind words or thoughtful deeds. Most importantly, my Mother is a Christian woman; her unwavering faith in God has never faltered. I have always believed that Mother has a direct telephone line to God; her prayers for her family and friends are constant and never go unanswered. She can sense what someone else needs, and she strives to fulfill that need with a helping hand, a loving heart. She is a pillar of strength, one who has traveled a road that was not always smooth, but she is a survivor and has taught me to follow her example.

Although we will have our differences, I would truly like to be the kind of woman Mother represents. I have loved her as a child at her knee when she first taught me to pray, and I love her now as a woman in my own right. I feel truly blessed that she was the one who gave me life.

Did I ever tell you you're my hero?
You're everything I would like to be.
I can fly higher than an eagle,
'cause you are the wind beneath my wings.

God bless you, Mom . . . I love you.
—Kym

Kymberly Twyman McEnheimer

To Nana:
Celia Bell Bagley
(1903-1978)

Long lean ebony limbs
>Never to embrace me

Gnarled, worn hands
>Never to caress me

Fire speckled legs so thin and straight
>Never to walk toward me

I'm missing you
I'm needing you
And memories cannot replace
What you were to me:
>A strong, proud stallion
>Head forever erect
>In a world that tried to wear you down
>A back that bore
>>the weight of a thousand days of sorrows, misgivings,
>>and rejection.

Yet, the tears fell only on the inside
Too proud to let them see
That you had feelings, too.
So tired, so worn
And yet you never fell

My Name is Kym

You never let those small shoulders droop
Until your eyes were closed
In the eternal sleep
Known only to those who had gone before you.
And they are the ones who embrace you now.
They are the ones who caress you now
They are the ones who dry the tears of joy
that fall freely down your enraptured face
For now you are in glory,
        and no one can hurt you,
No one can make you lean
        when you didn't want to bend.
No one can make you hurt
        when you gave all you had and no one understood.
I know you're smiling
        that special expression I
        carry in my dreams
And one day I want to be with you
        forever this time
        forever this time . . .

Kymberly Twyman McEnheimer

Six-year-old Kym with her Nana

A Letter to Nana—2

Dear Nana,

All I can say is how very much I miss you. It's been 14 years, and so much has happened since then. I know you've seen it all from your "window seat in heaven."

Please don't cry for me. I'll be alright somehow. I always hear that God doesn't give us more than we can bear. I believe that, though it's hard sometimes. But, through a lot of my grief, I find the light, and it makes me hold my head up, even when I don't want to. It gives me strength that I really didn't know I had. It keeps me keeping on.

I think of you, and so many griefs you bore, and yet you always stood tall. I often wish I had your courage, your strength. Maybe there's a little of it in me. I hope so. I often think about how much I've needed you over the years, just someone to talk to. And I know you live in my heart, now and always. So, I talk to you in prayer, in my dreams, and maybe it's you who bestows the strength to face all of this.

Thank you.

Look at Her

Soprano echoes through our little house

climbs the wall and bounce from the ceiling

— Look at her!

Love on a face of a thousand expressions as she smiles at me.

— Look at her!

In times of need, she's there to guide me. I've got a friend.

— Look at her!

That's right, look at her. I see through the coffee-colored skin, the
deep-set brown eyes and wisps of grey.

I have eyes to see through it all

At a rare and unique art that can only be my mother.

— Look at her!

Old House

A feel akin to you in some way or another.

Why, you've stood and watched me grow.

Invisible eyes saw me blossom from a little girl, running freely through your lawn, playing hide and seek in your room, crying little girls on starry nights, and swelling with pride upon a first graduation.

Yes, you've been there. You've seen it all.

What can I say, old house? I'm growing up and must take my leave.

Departing from a friend, a parent, a lover but I want you to know "I will always love you!"

The house where Kym grew up

Mother

My mother is like a rare pearl
You find only once in a lifetime,
and treasure always.
My mother is like a newly opened rose
delicate and fragrant,
Yet everlasting in its beauty.
My mother is special to everyone
whom she chances to touch,
sharing her gift of love
and bringing a smile to others.
My mother is strength and womanhood,
one to be admired,
one to be respected.
My mother is irreplaceable
in my heart,
for she has lit the candle of light
that glows in my eyes.
When I gaze into her face

I present my mother.

Kymberly Twyman McEnheimer

Birth on The Way

Yesterday I discovered the egg—an unfertilized life—
A stunted growth in which I had full
—control.
Today I revered the significance of being—
unique and alone . . . independent.
Tomorrow may reveal a revelation,
a rebirth of that being—
denied, postponed, and ignored.
The days to follow, the incomplete hours,
the unfulfilled seconds
may create a new discovery
of myself—of what I am about—
for I can feel the egg disintegrate within,
an urgent cry to develop,
yet I hear it not.

Sons

A little wonder
So soft and round
Folds of tenderness
and the scent of
small daisies in the rain.

The joy of it all
the wonderment
which needs no answer
Is all one could desire
Far passing the wildest dream
He is all there
and yet so much more
A part of life
entwined with my own.

Shaine Christopher 9/25/87

Kyle Everette 9/15/90

To Be Grown

It's difficult to be grown and act grown and impress others of our maturity when we don't know the meaning of grown in relation to ourselves.

To be grown is to behave in a respectable manner without the false airs that are misunderstood as acting grown when actually we are seen through the critical eyes of others as childish. To act grown is to display to the world an inner personality that doesn't need to be flaunted yet we mistake it for impression.

The meaning of grown surpasses the dictionary for only we can define it properly through our thoughts, words, and deeds and even so, every now and then we may stop, and wonder are we behaving in a grown-up manner. We'll never stop having doubts for who is grown enough to tell us the truth?

Bagley Family Reunion - Philadelphia

Bagley Family Reunion - Alabama

Kym

on

Love

Picture Stories

Michelle took one last look at the table before she went upstairs to change. She glanced at her wristwatch. Five o'clock. Just twenty more minutes.

Today was Kurt's, Michelle's husband's, birthday and she wanted everything to be pretty special. The dining room was decorated divinely to Kurt's taste. An array of selected flowers was placed in the two windows in elegant gold vases. The large white curtain had been drawn to give the room a shadowed glow from the dimly lighted chandelier hanging directly over the table. The table was set for two with tall wine glasses (already filled) in front of each plate. The best silverware was arranged on the table beside the embroidered cloth napkins. The main dish, a French souffle, was set upon the table by Louisa (the hired maid) as she busily went around the table making small adjustments for the perfection of the table.

The doorbell sounded at exactly twenty minutes after five. Louisa hurried to the kitchen in order not to be seen. Michelle hurried down the stairs to the door. Her long black hair was pinned up in a French roll with tendril curls hanging on the sides. She busily clipped on tiny green earrings as she hurried to answer the door. With each movement of her long slender body, the pea-green chiffon gown swayed gently behind her.

"You look very lovely, Michelle," Louisa complimented her as she passed the kitchen door.

Michelle smiled gracefully and opened the door. Kurt, a tall, dark man, stood expectantly at the door.

He kissed his wife gingerly as he stepped inside to put his big black briefcase in the closet. As he was hanging up his coat, Kurt caught a whiff of the French souffle. He smiled again at Michelle who stood behind him, waiting. She took him by the hand and led him to the dining room. His eyes grew round in surprise when he saw the table.

"Happy birthday, darling," Michelle whispered softly.

He looked at her, his eyes soft and kind. There were no words spoken, just the sweet taste of his lips on hers.

I'm In Love

I'm in love with a face, a figure, not my own
I'm in love with a dream, a feeling unexpressed
I'm in love with a life that I never understood
I'm in love with a vision I cannot touch
I'm in love with all there is to love
And there is as much reality
Here within me to make me smile.

I've Never Made Love

I've never made love like a woman to a man
From a woman, from that man
I've never felt love like I should
like he should and I should,
he should, too.

It's a matter of experience
I just ain't got it to boast about.
I don't need it; it will only create more dust
To brush away on cloudy days
When I need love, for love, with love,
Feeling love, no love . . .
For me!

Life, Love, and Being Me

I've got so much to learn about life, about love, about being me
I've got so much to do with life, with love, about being me
I've got so much to see with life, with love, with being me
How much time?
How much effort does it take?
How will I know when life and love entwined comes
knocking at my door?
When I don't know how to be myself.

Love Can't Pay the Bills

Love can't pay the bills
Love can't face the consequences
Love can't ease the hurt I feel
Or dry the tears I shed
Love can only offer itself
Four little words
That don't mean much except . . .
when there is an "I" and a "You"
and whispered in your deep, seductive voice
Mm-m-m, I love you.

Kymberly Twyman McEnheimer

Bad Influence

Children see and hear so much on television
that they can't possibly understand it all (at least I hope not).
Crime and violence are colorful examples that become feature
attractions for a young, developing mind.
Sex and use of bad language only corrupt innocent minds that should
not be exposed to such at an early age.
Will our sweet and beautiful children grow up and plot murders, rape
innocent victims, and plan robberies? (I hope not.)
(Let's hope not together)

Love Word

Love is a wonderful word that stretches and unwinds,
        but never shrinks.
    Love is an endless maze that has no entrance and no exit,
        but the middle is so very special.
    Love turns me around in circles,
        has me doing flips and wild turnabouts—but never dizzy.
    Love is a special feeling, a satisfactory dream,
        but there's no dictionary deep enough to express
What I have in my heart,
      what I can open my mouth and say
         that love is aglow
            in sky blue for us.
And love is . . .
      Aw heck, why not come right out and say?
       I

          Love
             You!

Baby—now, today, tomorrow, and eternity!

Kymberly Twyman McEnheimer

Love, Be My Guest

Well, it's just about over now.
Love's left me for the day
It's gone where all loves go
That do not have a heart
To take shelter

Love, be my guest
Come to me another time
Stay awhile longer and really
Let me know where you're coming from
Where you've been all my life

Making Love

Making love is kinda special
  It needs no questions
And doesn't depend on answers
  Making love is an unquenchable hunger
A never-sought problem
  That lies hidden in the heart
Making love is mysterious
  You never are prepared
But lay back and let it happen
  Let what is, what are
Let be, Let will
  Let me be with you
    And create . . .
    And discover . . .
      And make sweet, harmonized love.

Paralyzed

I love you and there's nothing more to say.
What's wrong can be corrected,
what's right can be left alone
but what's love can remain love.
For baby, I cannot feel anything
but the numbness of your love.
I've been paralyzed into a passionate pleasure and . . .
there's nothing more to say.

Passionate Pisces

The Passionate Pisces is warm and satisfying.
The Passionate Pisces has sought the love
that I never knew existed within.
The Passionate Pisces captured the glow of a radiant love,
and gave it to me so that I may be warm and satisfied.
The Passionate Pisces receives from me all that I have within.
He takes and I give; he has and I need
and it all smooths out into a passionate pleasure from
the Pisces with peace.

Past Loves

Reminiscing about past loves,
what's happened to them?
What's happened to me?
I am a woman, they are men.
I carry the seed for them
to help sow and plant
a child springs forth.
And he will remember his past loves,
but will he cry for mine?

Sugar-Coated Love

Sugar-coated love's glitter is scraped away
with a dirty fingernail.
Sugar coated love loses its taste
after the first bite.
Sugar-coated love is transparent—
a sheer protection from reality.
Our love is unreal, a mere fantasy
that is unreal even to a
sugar-coated heart like mine.

Sugar

Sugar tastes good on your good on your pillow lips
Sugar tastes sweet on your baby soft body
Sugar tastes like sweet love when you're making me yours,
Sugar, baby, love . . .

Tortured Heart

Lovers holding hands today
took a stab at my heart
(Innocently of course, but I still felt the pain).
That look between them,
I tried to turn away from,
but it haunted me.
I couldn't escape until my heart had been
tortured to the max.

World Without Love

It's a wild world without love
Untamed hearts prowl around and bite;
It hurts

It's a fierce world without love
Unfriendly hearts stab at my smiles;
It hurts

The jungle is dangerous
I have no weapons
Love me, please—
so I can fight back . . .

Boundaries

Pain without boundaries
Wandering aimlessly, purposefully
Through a ravaged mind
Forever in pursuit
seeking the blood to spill and expose.
Insatiable beyond the most minute imagination
Emptying the soul
And laughing at its shame
Daring a challenge
so confident in its conquest
The naked truth . . .
The enemy lives on.

The Tears

A cry in the dark
Echoes only in the mind
No one can hear
No one can care
Silent tears cursing a
Ravaged, faceless alien
Belonging to no one
For there is only the silence
And the rejection of the multitude
Is too intense to comprehend.   Kym

I understand your cries and the silent tears that fall —
in the silence of your pain.
I reach out to touch you . . . as a gesture of comfort
for I, too, know the emptiness
that dwells within your heart
I feel the rejection and know the deep cuts left behind
But the intensity of your love is where we first failed . . .
When we gave ourselves completely to one who could not
comprehend
the depth of our love.
Continue to love . . . but never give up ourselves in the process.

Pain without boundaries

Wandering aimlessly, purposefully
Through a ravaged mind
Forever in pursuit
seeking the blood to spill and expose
Insatiable beyond the most minute imagination
Emptying the soul
And laughing at its shame
Daring a challenge
so confident in its conquest
The naked truth . . .
The enemy lives on.   Kym

> *Pain has no boundaries when the enemy rules—*
> *The challenge lies within our own soul—*
> *Where we will begin to fill its emptiness*
> *With a love that soars*

Escape

To escape the lion
who preys its victim
is a dangerous feat
that seems impossible
to accomplish.
To escape its thunderous roar,
clasping ears, squeezing shut
the eyes to hold in the tears.
It cannot be done
without a miracle—source unknown—
for the lion has eyes
that do not see
but sear through the heart.
For the lion has ears
that do not hear,
but mock its victim's mind.
For the lion has a mouth
which does not eat,
but engulfs and devours
without thought.

Fallen Stars

Wishing upon fallen stars
of short-lived sparkle
A glimmer of what may have been
A shimmer of what should have been
No more to shine
Faded. Silence.
An eerie glow inside the
dying heart
Be still and listen
to the calm
It speaks the truth
I didn't want to hear
It casts the light
Upon what I didn't want to see
It cries the anguish
I didn't want to feel
It leaves me alone
To wait
To die.

Nightmare

Drifting through a nightmare
Terrifying images of the mind
Torture for the heart
Restlessness for the soul
The light has faded
and the path is not so clear.
But it must be there somewhere, somehow,
some day . . .

Wishes

Wishes are for children
who dare to dream
and know someone will
make them realities.
Wishes are for the innocent
who haven't lived with pain, hurt, and frustration
for then there are no
wishes except to die in peace.

A Box of Chocolates

Black Heritage

Makes ya look at your hands.
Feel your, stare deeply, darkly into your eyes.
Makes ya feel like moving.
Dancin' to a beat that has traveled far across the waves.
Makes ya look at your mama in a way that you never did before
Makes you wanna be held by your strong, black daddy, wanna kiss
Grandma.
I wanna shout, I gotta shed some held back tears.
I wanna listen. I can hear them cries of my brothers and sisters.
It's in my blood, that's a part of me.
Out there in the unmarked graves.
It's me. Can't you see?
I wanted to be there; I wanted to feel it for myself,
But oh, that feeling has not died.
It's traveled some miles, swam some rivers and it's finally hit home in
my bosom.
Mmm, I can feel it rock,
I can feel it swell it's there, I just had to look the other way.
Nowhere chil'? I can't turn my back on my bea—u—tiful . . .
black heritage!

No sir!

Kymberly Twyman McEnheimer   121

Bridge

I wish there was some bridge
to gap that dangles
forever before us.
Taunting at times
primarily dormant
rearing its deceptive head
only when I need you
which isn't often,
because I've pretended for so long
not to.
And so, the years pass
from childhood to teen
to womanhood and beyond
and it becomes something
you just don't dwell on
at least not anymore.

Christmas

Christmas has skipped away its holiday glow.
The tall evergreens bend under their own weight,
and the wind echoes across the valley.
Listen! It seems to mourn
with paths made by the scholars,
The philosophers, the poets—
footprints that contain assurance, confidence,
treads of steel.
The pale brick buildings cluster about the hand,
as if huddling from the knowledge that forms within.
The people, they're here for a goal.
I pray that they react it.

Crooked Carol

Crooked Carol is defiant and loud
Crooked Carol says, "Ain't nobody gonna mess with me!"
Crooked Carol bears a masculine strut as
she sasheys on down the alley.
Crooked Carol's bulging black buttons are closed.
Her Afro wig has been removed and the
tangled beads of black heritage are scattered about her oval head.
Crooked Carol lies straight now.
Satin and chiffon crisp, cool sheet, flowers and soft music.
Yessir! Crooked Carol lies straight now!
She's met her match.
And from what I hear, it was some battle!

Lonely Hearts

Lonely hearts find a friend
in the darkness of despair.
Groping, yet never grasping,
seeking, yet never finding.
lonely hearts find a comfort
in the tears that stain pillows,
puffed eyes and a look of woe begone.
Perhaps it is a sad destiny,
perhaps it is a bitter fate
Yet understand, it brings
no peace
no joy
only a silent rage
that knows no quiet.

Now Is Not

Now is not the time,
nor the day, nor the hour.
Now is not the time,
nor the minute, nor the second.

Now is not for me,
for us.
And so we wait,
so we do not.
Now is not for us.
Now is not our time.

Kym with Donna, her lifelong friend

Once More

If I could speak your name
Once more
If I could feel your embrace
Once more
If I could touch your body
Once more
I would find my peace.

If it is but a word for those
Who regret
If it but a feeling for those
Who lament
The torture is real
The reality is now
The silence is unbearable
Places.

It's lonely in HELL, but how should I know?
It's peaceful in HEAVEN, but who says so?
Places between places, I want to be
Here in the middle where I can sink nor rise,
But bounce quietly from side to side.

Secrets

Secrets bear the burden of a trouble heart.
Ripping it into small pieces,
prey for the vultures of life to frolic
among the ruin, and laugh.
It's an eerie sound,
it pierces the soul exposing old wounds
for all to all to see, as some turn away in disbelief.
And others turn to face the truth,
my secrets are yours,
and together we must pay the price.

Someone's Watching Me

Someone's watching me . . .
> Somebody's pulling me through.

Is it you, God?

I feel a guiding hand.
I feel a comfortable protection.

Is it you, God?

> Is it you that's helping me grow
> the way that's right for me?

Is it you, God?

> If it is, I wish to say
> humbly with the biggest smile
> I can muster,

> Thank you, with love.

My Name is Kym

Sometimes

Sometimes I feel the sun, but there is no window
Sometimes I hear the drums, but all is dark and silent
Sometimes I'm here, but I am always confused
Sometimes is just a word and the dictionary is wide open.

Trembling

I stood trembling at the path to glory
My feet would not move, my legs wobbled in fear.
Don't push me, I'm afraid to take the first step.
Lead me to glory land rang the spiritual
Lead me humble.
I can't go, but there's nowhere to turn.
Hold my hand, guide me through
The barrier of my mind.
I'm gonna make it!
I can see that gleaming cross
Smiling down and me.

Visions

The vision is enveloped in a cloud
Silver-lined with jagged edges
Missing pieces, interruptions,
Pregnant pauses without rhyme or reason
Escape the chaos
To better see the light
Yet it is blinding
And not as friendly as once imagined
So, perhaps it is better to keep hiding
A safe haven among warriors
Not a friend waiting with outstretched arms
Not a lover seeking warmth and security
Only the cold silence
The rude awakening
Of what once was a peace of mind.

Your Worst

If your worst is not your best,
then sit back and don't complain.
Excuses to cover up—lack of time,
distraction, tiredness—
they crumble like cookie crumbs
on the wooden floor,
left for the black ants to pick up.
Your worst should speak a lot for the best
of your ability.
Why? There's no distinction.
Everything you do should make you
feel good
feel satisfied.
Say, "I've done a good job."
Don't let the ants be the only
ones who have the picnic.

For All Seasons of Love with You

One day at a time. That's all I can handle.
    ~~ Right Now ~~
One dream at a time. I've got a lot of life ahead.
    ~~ Right Now ~~
One minute I can see it all so clear
      and ~~ Right Now ~~ it vanishes
  Before my eyes!
One second was all it took as my one
   day, my one dream,
        was stripped away
          by reality
            right now . . .

How Terribly Sad

How terribly sad that she should scare me so.
Those eyes that looked upon me with love,
such a tender motherly love.
Those eyes, dark with anger, a punishment
in itself as they bore through flesh crying for my repentance.
And now I cannot face them
I cannot pour out the deep secrets of my heart
Oh how I ache so inside
My heart cries bitterly
And my tongue lies silent, a threatening menage
Which may one day cover my throat and choke . . .
I'm afraid . . . oh God, give me courage.
I'm burning with anxiety, my heavy chest heaves loudly
as it shifts its load.
Oh, let me speak, let me cry out to Mama.
It must be done and I can't face it.
I'll stammer, I'll stutter, tears will be my absent words.
I can't . . . she scares me so.
It's strange after all these years,
I cannot talk to a woman I love.
Is it love? If so, then why can't I speak
from my heart without feeling the clutches
of fear lock my mind?

Parasite

Parasite . . .
Shuffled along through time
Days become an eye to blink
Years are merely uncouth yawns
Take a stretch.
Detach.
Reach out and snatch a day to call
my own.

Today's Unique

Today's been unique, I've mastered another
step in life.
My goal, my long-awaited dream has
drawn near
to wrap its comforting arms about me
and say softly,
"You've done well; I'm proud."
I need those words so badly.
They offer encouragement.
That's what counts
as I peer into tomorrow's shadow.

Inner Feelings

What perfect place to express my inner feelings,
what more normal surroundings,
such a beautiful atmosphere in which to create.
The time has come, the hour is now upon me.
the minutes of the day have divided my time—waiting
a time . . . an hour in which I tend to a daily devotion.
It is one of writing, one of which my thoughts
know no boundaries;
I am free, my inspiration has come.
And now I must convey my most secret emotions.
May they burst forth in such a flurry
that the wind scatters them about the land,
perhaps to touch a lone stranger traveling in the
snow or land softly upon the brow of a mischievous
child whose eyes dance in the night.
I want to spread, branch out and touch the world,
to give the gift of life—mentally
to share the knowledge of love—mentally
to transfer the dreams of tomorrow—mentally.
I'm open, strip me naked of my thoughts,
drain the succulent passion for words,
drink, eat and come back for seconds,
for I am always here.
Alone by the fire, the chilling wind from an
open window beats upon my back.
Yet I am warm,
my heart is warm,
my love I give to you is warm,
so, cuddle close . . .

Kymberly Twyman McEnheimer

An Awakening Author

To whom it may inspire:

Writers are extremely strange people. Very few individuals can comprehend what scribbles about in their ever-composing heads. They are completely dominated by an endless string of words that frequently knots around their necks as they bend relentlessly over battered typewriters. A poet inhabits a mysterious maze of rhymes, phrases, and run-on sentences. He or she constantly satisfies the uncontrollable need to compose and create images that are often puzzling to the 'uninspired reader.'

A writer of fiction or plays alienates himself in a secret room filled with incomplete ideas and outlines dangling from the ceiling or balancing dangerously on a crowded shelf. The art of writing is the breadcrumbs that feed the hungry creator. A starving writer discovers himself devoured by unexpressed feelings and withers away. The art of composing is a sacred gift from the soul that must be nurtured and encourage to develop. Is this why I'm here? Perhaps I am a nurtured seed, destined to share my gift with the world. I need your help in unraveling my tangled thoughts emerging in the dawn of free expression … I just want to be: strange, alienated, or dominated. That is, this is me and my creation.

What Self-Realization Means to Me

I view the concept of self-realization as a winding, mysterious road along which all of us must travel in search of the personal meanings of life. To me, self-realization parallels with revelation—widening the eyes to capture the sights, sounds, pleasures, and tragedies of everyday life. There are secrets hidden within all of us, and self-realization becomes a means in which these hidden feelings and thoughts are revealed to the individual in order for us to gain a tighter grip on reality.

Self-realization is a traumatic process which propels a person along that road, and sometimes they stumble or fall, or are even forced to take a few steps backwards in order to keep moving. Self-realization is a direction, neither up nor down, in nor out, but a movement, a force that drives the individual, guiding them toward their destiny. I can imagine everyone traveling along this universal road, not knowing what lies beyond each bend, but to me, it is realizing that you are an individual—a unique being walking alone.

Self-realization is not simply following the crowd, allowing others to pick you up when you fall, or push and pull you along when you're weary and desire rest. For the individual, self-realization begins when you make that decision to stop, to allow others on that road of life to pass you by. Then, you are thinking and acting for yourself. Self-realization lies in the will to say, "No, I'm not going to be like everyone else. I am a person unto myself, and I make my own decisions."

As mentioned before, self-realization is a difficult process that is not achieved or discovered in a day or a few years. It is continuous, yet never repetitious, and each day as I grow and develop into a more unique being, self-realization becomes more obvious. Of course, it is not something that is realized with age or maturity, but simply a daily awareness of the young woman crying out inside my very soul to be unique.

I feel that self-realization has no definite end, or at least not a state of being that can be finalized, (for example, as when one reaches adulthood at 21). Sometimes I believe that I am just beginning to realize who I am, where I am going, and what I must do in life; and at other times, I feel as though I have not begun at all. Self-realization is truly a means of stepping outside of yourself and conducting a critical self-evaluation. It involves making corrections, adjustments, and realizing and accepting faults.

But the most crucial question that I ask myself when pondering the concept of self-realization is "who am I?" I feel that this is the base, the first road that must be crossed before the journey along the others. For me, it is the most difficult to define. Too often people think of themselves in terms of their capabilities, physical strengths, where they will be tomorrow, what others think of them, and the images projected from the types of people they associate with. But the question of who they actually are remains and is sadly ignored or lost in a long list of trivialities.

I thought extremely hard about who I truly am, and what type of person I have become in my 22 years. However, I was not disappointed in a failure to honestly answer the question. I chose to expose the answer in other ways, such as by evaluating my moral standards, past experiences, and personal dreams and expectations for the future. By surrounding the question, I was able to gain a broader perspective of myself and discover emotions and thoughts that I was not previously aware of. Thus, self-realization became a personal revelation—a wealth of pleasant surprises.

I agree that self-realization is grasping a sense of oneself. Once this has been achieved, it remains and becomes a natural part of daily growth. There are difficulties in dealing with this initial awareness of the self, and sometimes I find it overwhelming. Just when I feel that I can move forward, having gained deeper insights into my integral being, "things" happen, and I find myself stuck in the same spot, uprooted and confused, or even pushed back to begin all over again. When I speak of 'things," I am referring to personal traumas, such as dealing

My Name is Kym

with parents who still think of me as their little girl; a girlfriend who doesn't agree with a particular point of view; a boyfriend over the precious heartaches of love; or even whirlpools within myself that seem to spread wider when coping with term papers, final examinations, and making decent grades. All of these "things" pass with time, and it becomes extremely crucial to maintain a sense of self, if only for reasons of stability!

As I pondered over my final thoughts on self-realization, I have become increasingly aware of how far I have yet to travel along the road of life. Sometimes, it is the unknown that we fear the most. I worry about how I will deal with a problem or a situation that fatefully lies in all our futures. Possessing a sense of oneself restores confidence, and perhaps that is one of the essential ingredients of self-realization. It is knowing where you have come from based on past experiences and knowledge and employing these insights as keys to unlock the doors of the future.

Wake Up World

People today are swept up in a world of many different things, different cultures, societies, and different worlds. As strange as it may seem, man is drawing away from himself. So many ideas occur in every person's mind to keep one man from being like another. Who knows, one day man may not be here. Slowly men are becoming apart, different in a world that they struggle to become independent where it is too crowded. Man governs his own life, his own ideas and ways of living which makes this seem even more true.

Why do we struggle to get more? It seems man is always crying out, more! More! More! Can't we be happy with what we have? Greed, prejudice, and selfishness all blend in together in the fight. These keep man apart and will continue to do so. There seems no hope to get out of the dizzy circle which keeps spinning, spinning around stretching out its long, octopus arms sweeping us up into the unpleasant world I don't see why we struggle. What good does it do? To become better than another? To be more important? Why? Why? There are no answers, no cry of help or mercy. Is it too late to free man from those long, grasping arms that bound him in chains? Wake up world! Why do we kill? Wake up world! Why do we hate? Wake up world! Why do we fight to be different? Wake up world! Open your ears and stop! Look! And Listen! Open up your eyes and look around you. Look what is happening, what is happening to your world, my world, our world.

By Kym Twyman

Kymberly Shawn Twyman McEnheimer

Epilogue

Shaine McEnheimer

Hello, my name is Shaine McEnheimer and I'm Kymberly's oldest son. Mother passed away when I was 13 years old. I was very young along with my younger brother Kyle and it was very hard for us to fully understand what was happening at the time. I was graduating from middle school and ready to start high school for the first time. We lived with Mother before she passed, and we had a great childhood. As a kid, I know she cared about us deeply and made sure her two boys were taken care of. There is not a day goes by that I don't think about Mother and what she did for us as we were growing up. I will always love and miss her dearly and I know she is looking down on us with a smile, knowing her two boys are all grown up and doing the right things in life.

As we grew up, Grandmother always told me Mother left behind writings and poetry that spoke a lot about her as person and how she saw the world at that time. Now at 33 years old and with more life experience, I'm extremely grateful she has kept and compiled Mother's writings not only for my brother and me, but also for you to enjoy and continue the legacy Mother left behind. I'm blessed to be able to remember my mother through her writings and that brings happiness to my heart. I hope her writings brought some of that same happiness to you.

I love you, Mom, and thank you for everything! I promise I won't let you down.

Kyle McEnheimer

My name is Kyle Everette McEnheimer, and my mother's name is Kymberly Shawn Twyman-McEnheimer. Although our heavenly Father called Mother back to Heaven, it continues to be a pleasure for myself and others to continue to get to know her through her writings and illustrations. It calls to mind what is found in Exodus 23:20: "Behold, I send an Angel before thee, to keep thee in the way, and to bring thee into the place which I have prepared." As I grow older, I understand that those who have departed from this physical existence still and will always reside in a spiritual existence outside of our human view, where God has prepared a table for my mother in His presence.

I love Mother dearly and I am honored to be called her child and God's child—I smile at the inevitable day ahead when I can see her face again. I miss Mother equally as much as the love she had and still has for her family and friends. I pray that her writings have blessed and touched your heart because I know that is what she would have wanted.

Thank you to my Grandmother, Juanita Bagley-Twyman, for her many hours of dedication and love to gather and compile this collection of my mother's work. *"Thank you, Grandma!"*

Love,
Kyle McEnheimer